Kevin and Lotty were going to play on the rocks. They went down the lane. They came to the gate. They bent down to creep under it.

"Moo ... moo ...." Oh no!   There was a big brown cow behind the hedge.

"Moo, moo," said the big brown cow.

Kevin did not like cows.

"I am not going past that big brown cow," he said. "We shall have to find another way to the rocks."

The two little dogs went down the lane until they came to a gap in the hedge. They could see the rocks. "Now, let's run to the rocks," said Lotty.

"Grrr … grr …." Oh no! There was a big brown dog behind the hedge. The dog was growling. "Grrr … grrr … grr."
Kevin did not like big dogs.

"I am not going past that big brown dog," said Kevin. "We shall have to find another way to the rocks." So the little dogs went down the lane.

Soon they came to some trees. They could see the rocks at the other side of the trees. "Now, let's run to the rocks," said Lotty.

"Tu-whit tu-whoo." Oh no! A brown owl flew down from a tree. It made Kevin howl. "Ow, ow. I am not going past that brown owl," he said.

Lotty was cross with Kevin now. "Then I shall go to play on the rocks by myself," she said. She ran off to the rocks to play by herself.

Kevin sat down on the grass. He felt all alone. Suddenly, he saw a big brown cow, a big brown dog and a brown owl. Oh no! What will Kevin do now?

"ow"

cow

now

down

brown

owl

howl

growling